D0597640

FOR YOUR OWN PROTECTION

For Ben Wolf, my father

Library of Congress Cataloging in Publication Data
Cobb, Vicki. For your own protection.
Includes index. Summary: Describes various photographic methods that can reveal natural
phenomena, very small or distant objects, or events that happen too quickly to be
discernible to the naked eye. 1. Photography — Scientific applications — Juvenile literature.
[1. Photography—Scientific applications] I. Title. TR692.C62 1989   778.3   89-2342
ISBN 0-688-08787-6   ISBN 0-688-08788-4 (lib. bdg.)

FOR YOUR OWN PROTECTION

STORIES SCIENCE PHOTOS TELL

BY VICKI COBB

LOTHROP, LEE & SHEPARD BOOKS   NEW YORK

QUICK AS A WINK

Stick a pin in a balloon. Pop! Air bursts out of the pinhole, tearing the balloon and making a loud sound. Within four-hundredths of a second your eyes close. The blink happens so quickly it seems almost instantaneous. Every hearing person reacts to the sound of a balloon burst, or any loud, sudden noise, exactly the same way. This reaction is called the startle reflex. You do it automatically, without thinking. The startle reflex is your body's way of protecting your eyes, your most important sense organs, from injury.

This picture captures the speed of the startle reflex. The rushing air has torn the balloon and produced the sound that causes the eyes to blink. But the balloon has not yet had time to collapse. The photograph was made with the use of a rapidly flashing light called a stroboscope, or strobe for short. The balloon was hooked up to a trigger that turned on the strobe when the balloon burst. The photo was made in a pitch-dark laboratory with the camera shutter open. The image was caught on the film when the strobe flashed.

Other threats in the environment besides loud noises can affect your well-being. The scientific photos in this book tell the story of some of these threats and some of the ways you protect yourself. The photos are a fascinating way of gaining insight into some very familiar things.

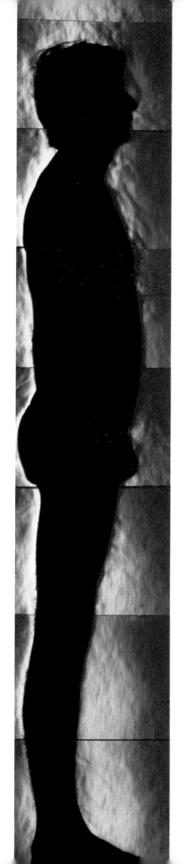

COLD

A special type of picture taken by a schlieren camera reveals a plume of warm air rising like a flame almost six feet above your body. Schlieren photography was invented in Germany about one hundred years ago. It was used to detect streaks in glass lenses. The word *Schlieren* means "streaks" in German. About twenty years ago, a scientist discovered that schlieren photography could reveal moving air.

Warm air rising from your body carries away not only heat, but also the hundreds of thousands of dead skin cells that are continually being shed. Heat constantly moves from your warm body to the cooler surrounding air. How fast you lose heat depends on how much colder than your body the air is and what kind of clothing you are wearing.

Your body generates heat, which is lost through your skin. Like those of other warm-blooded animals, your body works to maintain a constant internal temperature regardless of how cold or hot the air is. In a healthy person, this temperature is 98.6 degrees Fahrenheit. Heat is lost at different rates from different parts of the body, so some body surfaces are cooler than others.

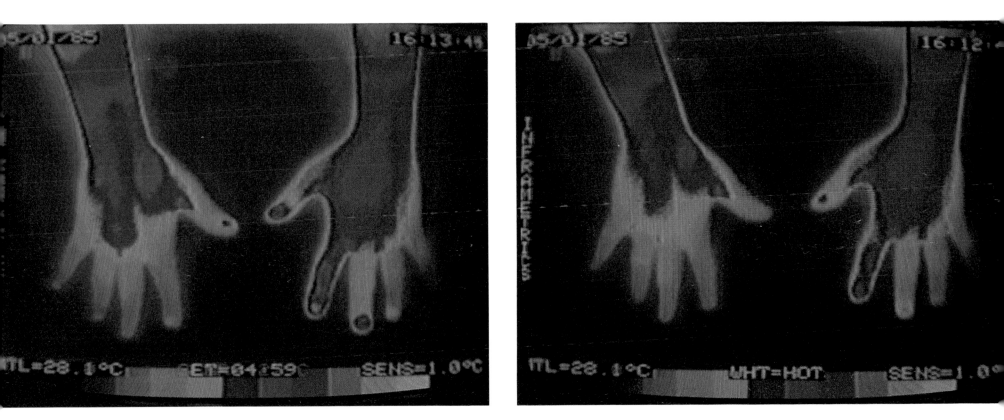

Thermography is a kind of scientific photography that shows the different temperature areas in different colors. In the thermograms showing the backs of a girl's hands, there is a color code running along the bottom. The colors from left to right indicate temperatures running from cooler to warmer. Reading the thermograms tells us that the fingers are the coldest part of the hands and that the wrists and arms are warmer. These thermograms were taken one minute apart. The temperature of the girl's left index finger warmed up by about one degree after she was told to "think hot."

GERMS

Infections and disease are often caused by certain ultra-tiny living things, bacteria and viruses, that can only be seen through a microscope. The scanning electron microscope uses a beam of electrons, like the ones that create your television picture, to show highly magnified details of the surfaces of microscopic objects. This is a scanning electron micrograph, called an SEM for short, of bacteria on the enamel surface of a tooth, magnified thirty-one thousand times. SEMs are always black and white but may be colored later, like this one, to enhance the image. A mixture of the round, yellow *Streptococcus mutans* bacteria with sugars and other carbohydrates forms plaque, which sticks to the enamel surface of teeth.

Tooth enamel is the hardest material produced by the body. Perfect teeth have been found in skulls buried for thousands of years. Yet the bacteria in plaque produce an acid from sugars that can eat through tough enamel to create cavities. For protection against cavities, cut down on sweets, brush and floss regularly to remove plaque, and see your dentist to repair small cavities before they develop into serious decay problems.

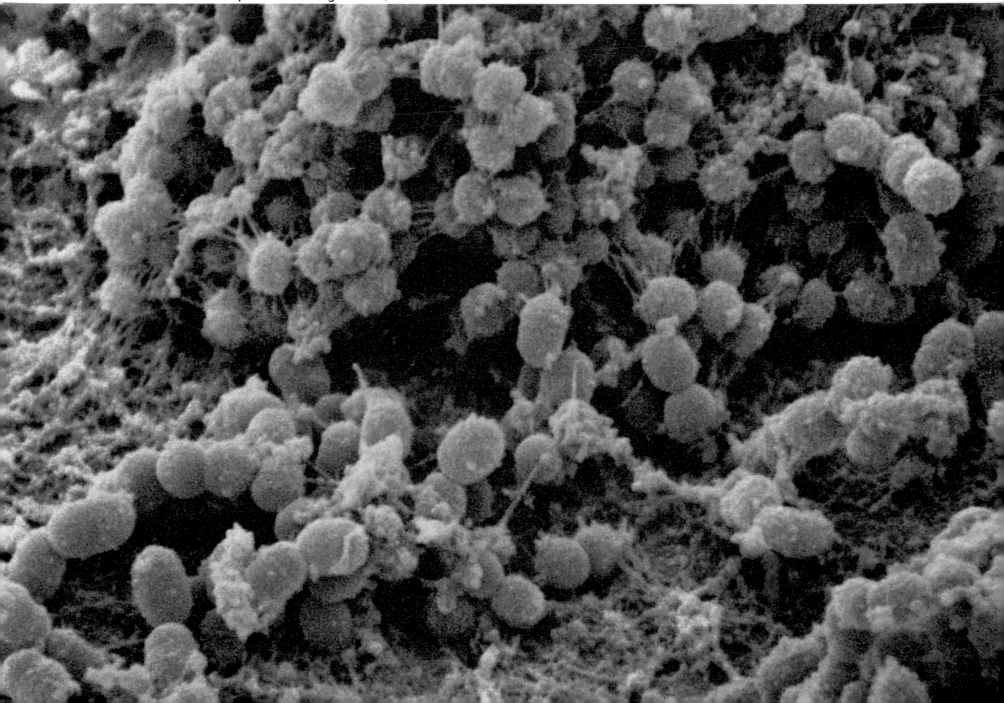

Plaque bacteria magnified 31,000 times.

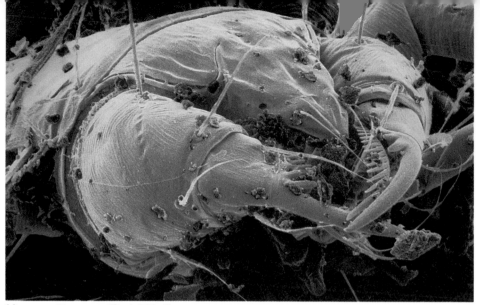

House mite magnified 551 times.

DUST

Skin cells shed by people and pets wind up as part of the dust on the surfaces of a home. Pollen grains, fragments of fibers, mold spores, and parts of dead insects add to the mix. Although dust may look lifeless and dry to you, it also contains tiny house dust mites that thrive by feeding on discarded skin cells. House dust mites have four pairs of legs and are distant cousins of spiders. They are so small that they can only be seen under a microscope. They live mostly in carpets and beds. The average double bed may contain two million of them. House dust mites don't need to drink water. They get water from their food and from the air. They do well when the relative humidity is between 60 and 80 percent. They are found in all homes all over the world, except in very dry climates.

The mite in this SEM is a house mite, a slightly larger relative of the house dust mite. It is shown surrounded by dust from a vacuum cleaner, collecting skin cells. The house mite feeds on groceries, furniture stuffing, and wallpaper paste, as well as skin cells. House mites and house dust mites are harmless to people, but their waste products can cause allergic reactions. Also, bacteria are found wherever there are living things, and some bacteria can be harmful. So dusting regularly and keeping your house clean gives you some protection from these hazards.

House dust magnified 182,600 times.

THE SNEEZE

What happens when you inhale dust or some other irritating substance? The hairs in your nose trigger a reflex, a sneeze, to forcefully expel the undesirable material. When you sneeze, you first inhale air to inflate your lungs. Next, your air passages close as your diaphragm (the breathing muscle under your lungs) compresses the air to create higher pressure in your lungs. Then the air passages suddenly open and the air literally explodes outward, carrying droplets of watery mucus from the lining of the nose and windpipe.

A sneeze exiting a nose has been clocked at slightly more than a hundred miles an hour. It contains perhaps five thousand droplets, and it can travel twelve feet. A cough is similar to a sneeze except that the irritating material is located lower down in the windpipe. The rushing air of a cough comes only out of the mouth.

This high-speed strobe photo captures an image of the sneeze droplets as they emerge from the nose. The scientist who took the photo tried using pepper to create a sneeze, but it didn't work. This sneeze was induced by pulling a hair from the nose. Don't try this yourself, because it can cause infection. Some of the material in sneeze droplets may contain germs that can spread sickness to others. So for the protection of others, cover your mouth and nose when you sneeze.

SKIN

Your skin is a close-fitting, seamless suit of armor, presenting a sealed layer of dead cells to the outside world. Bacteria that could cause infection live harmlessly all over this surface. Your skin acts as a raincoat and also protects you from harmful radiation from the sun. It helps keep you warm and cools you off. It is the source of your sense of touch.

Fingertip magnified 5 times.

Fingertip with sweat drops magnified 20 times.

The skin is made of two layers. The dermis is the deeper layer. It contains nerves, blood vessels, connective tissue, sweat glands, the roots of hairs, and the tiny muscles that cause goose bumps. The epidermis rests on top of the dermis and provides the shield of dead outer cells. It is composed of five layers. Its deepest layer is made up of rapidly dividing cells that are programmed to fill up with a tough protein and die. The outermost layer of dead cells is about twenty-five to thirty cells thick. It is these cells that are constantly being shed like scales.

Although you can feel pressure, temperature, and pain through skin all over your body, the fingertip is one of the most sensitive places. This magnified color photograph shows the typical ridges of a fingertip that provide extra traction for holding on to things. The pattern of these ridges is unique for every individual. People can be identified by their fingerprints. The SEM shows drops of sweat that form from sweat glands in the ridges. Dirt clings to this oily sweat and leaves fingerprints on surfaces you touch. Since dirty fingers are a likely place to find bacteria, hand washing is an important health safeguard.

BLOOD CLOT

If the skin is cut or torn, the body's first line of defense against the outside world is broken. Blood is lost, and bacteria can now enter the body. So the skin must be able to repair itself. A wound triggers a series of events that ultimately heals the opening in the skin and keeps our armor intact.

The body's initial job after a cut or scrape is to plug the wound and stop the bleeding. Injured skin cells give off a chemical that starts the process immediately. Every drop of blood contains about fifteen million tiny platelets, which stick to the wound and form a temporary plug that slows blood loss. The platelets give off another chemical that combines with blood proteins in a series of steps that produces strings of fibrin, forming a network that traps red cells and creates a scab. In the case of a small cut, fibrin appears about two minutes after the injury.

This SEM is artificially colored. It shows fibrin as pink threads trapping red blood cells that are colored yellow. In real life the red cells are red and the fibrin is straw-colored.

After an injury white blood cells rush to the area to destroy any harmful bacteria that may have entered. Once the scab has formed, skin cells underneath grow toward each other to close the wound.

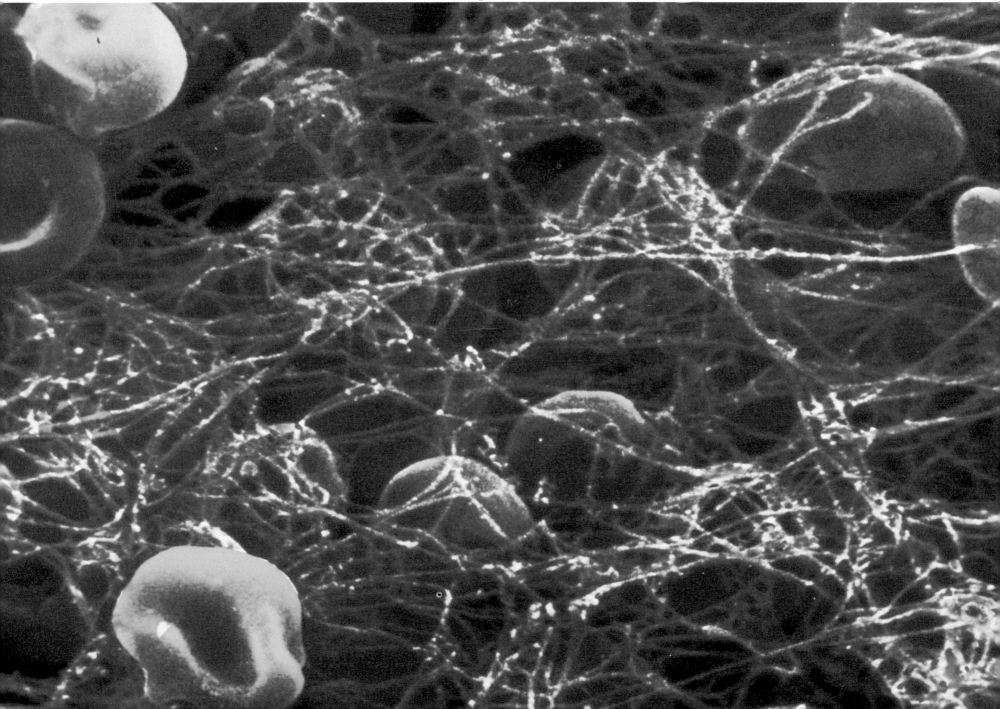

Blood clot with red cells trapped in fibrin magnified 10,750 times.

HAIR

Furry mammals have a coat of hair to protect them against cold temperatures. When an animal is chilled, its fur stands on end, increasing the amount of air trapped between hairs. This makes the fur better able to insulate against cold. The same reflex occurs when an animal is frightened or senses danger. The raised fur makes the animal appear larger than it actually is, which could cause an enemy to think twice before attacking.

In the process of evolution, human beings have lost the trait of heavy body hair, but our skin reacts to chill or fright nonetheless. Muscles contract, causing goose bumps that raise our body hair, but our hair is too fine to be a particularly effective means of keeping warm. Hair on the head, however, does offer some protection against cold and sun, and can cushion a blow.

Hair is made of a hard, scaly protein called keratin. Fingernails and toenails are made of the exact same stuff, but arranged differently. Every hair grows out of a group of living cells in the dermis called a hair follicle. The SEM shows a hair growing out of a hair follicle on the scalp. Notice that a dead skin cell clings to the side of the hair.

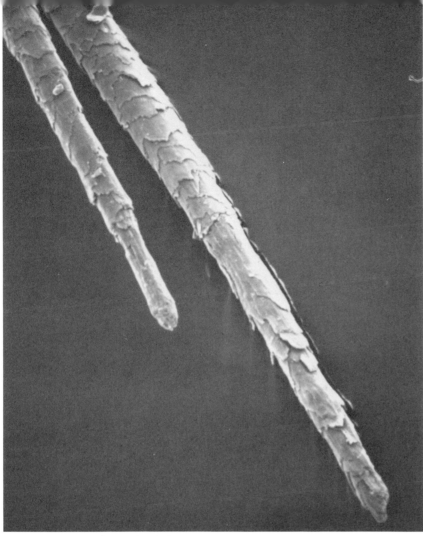

Eyelashes magnified 687.5 times.

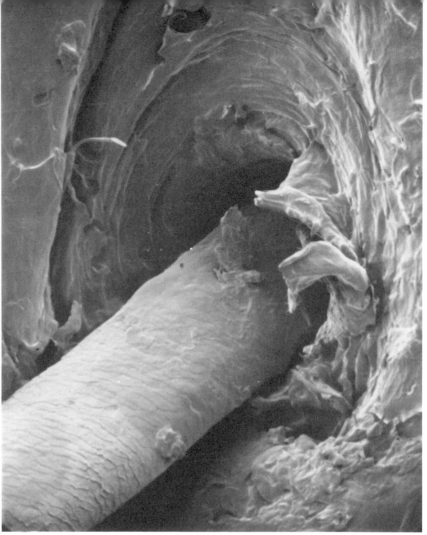

Hair growing from follicle magnified 462.5 times.

Eyebrows help protect the eyes by keeping sweat out of them. Eyelashes help shield the eyes and act as antennae, helping to sense objects near the eyes. The SEM shows the overlapping scales of eyelashes and their rounded ends, typical of uncut hair. Dead skin cells also cling to these hairs.

19

FIBERS

Since we have no furry coat to shield us from sun and cold, we have learned to use the fibers of plants and other animals for our own protection. These SEMs show different kinds of familiar fibers magnified 750 times.

Wool, cashmere, and mink are all animal fibers. Like human hair, they are made of tiny scales of layered protein. When wool fibers rub against one another, they form permanent tangles. This makes wool easy to spin into yarn. Wool is comfortable because it stretches. It is warm because air is trapped between its fibers. The surface resists water, but the fiber itself absorbs more water than any other natural fiber. As a result, wool outerwear provides great protection against cold and rainy weather.

◀ fine wool   ◀ coarse wool   ◀ cashmere   ◀ mink

Cotton fibers, which come from plants, look like flat, twisted ribbons. Cotton is about one-third as absorbent as wool, feels cool to the skin, and stands up well under laundering.

Silk fibers are spun by an insect, the silkworm, when it makes its cocoon. Silk is the thinnest natural fiber, does not wrinkle easily, and is soft, smooth, and warm.

Rayon is the first man-made fiber invented. It is made from wood pulp and cotton. It was first used in 1910 and is sometimes called artificial silk because its texture is similar to that of silk. Nylon, polyester, and other man-made fibers look smooth and very much alike in SEMs. Most man-made fibers do not absorb much water, and so they dry quickly. They are often used in blends with natural fibers to make cloth that has the advantages of both.

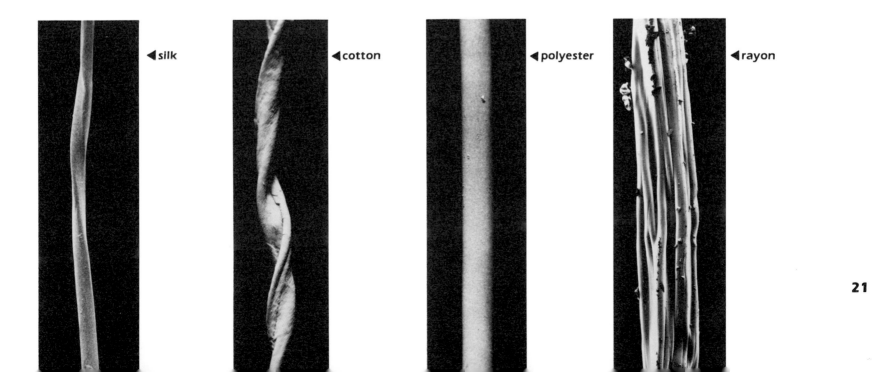

◀ silk   ◀ cotton   ◀ polyester   ◀ rayon

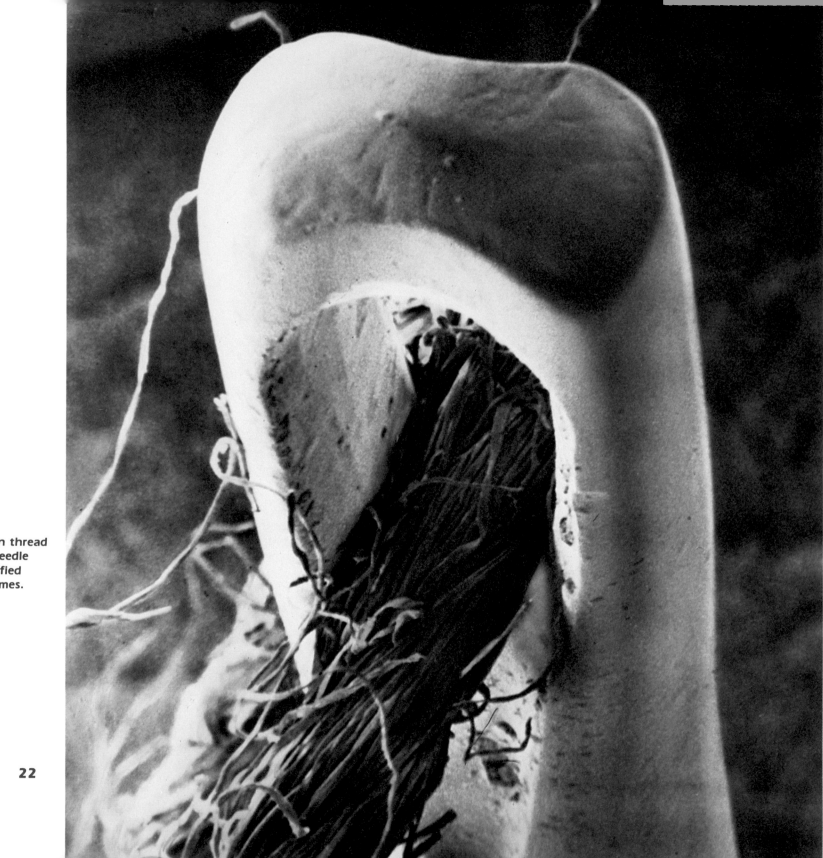

Cotton thread
and needle
magnified
160 times.

THREADS AND FABRIC

Single fibers are too small to be made into anything useful, so many tiny fibers are twisted together to form threads that can be woven or knitted into fabric. Fabrics can be cut and stitched to make clothing. The photo of a thread passing through the eye of a needle shows the many fibers of the thread, which give it a ropelike appearance.

The SEM on the left shows the dirty collar of a pure cotton shirt. The woven cotton threads are almost completely coated with grease, grime, and skin cells. The SEM on the right shows the same shirt after laundering. The "ring around the collar" has disappeared completely.

Dirty shirt collar magnified 37.5 times.

Shirt collar after laundering magnified 37.5 times.

OUTERWEAR

In addition to fabric, many other kinds of materials can protect us against cold and weather. We wear the furs of other animals and their preserved skins, known as leather. Rubber and vinyl plastics are useful waterproofing materials.

Leather can be a tough, waterproof material, depending on its thickness. These SEMs show two sides of a piece of leather. On the top side are pitted areas where hairs once grew. The un-

Skin side of leather magnified 360 times.

Suede side of leather magnified 360 times.

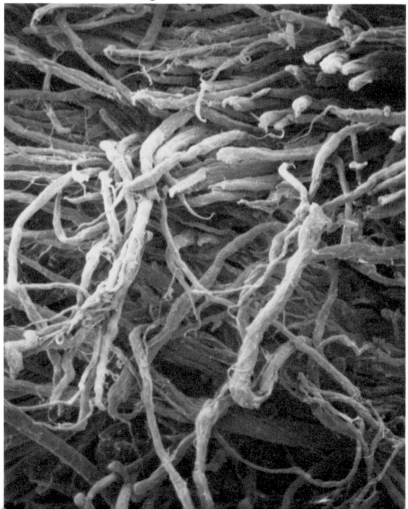

derside, or flesh side, is full of many protein fibers. The velvety surface of suede is made by neatly trimming these fibers.

Polyester fibers dry quickly, and very tight weaves can be fairly water-repellent. However, to be truly waterproof, polyester fabric should have a waterproof coating. This SEM shows a cross section of a piece of rubberized raincoat. It's easy to tell which side has been coated with rubber.

Rubberized nylon raincoat magnified 216 times.

25

ZIPPERS

Clothes are warmer and more comfortable to wear when they are fastened securely. Buttons, belts, and pins have served this purpose for centuries. The zipper, a modern fastener, was invented a hundred years ago by a man named Whitcomb Judson. A metal zipper is made of interlocking pieces fastened to two strips of tape. The tapes can be stretched into a curve to separate the individual fasteners. This is the job of the zipper's slide. As the slide moves, it curves the tapes so the teeth on one side can slip between those on the other. When the tape straightens out after the slide has passed, the teeth are interlocked and secure. The reverse slide spreads the teeth so they can unlock. The pic-

Locking teeth of metal zipper magnified 94 times.

ture on the left is a close-up of a metal zipper in the closed position.

The picture on the right is one-half of a nylon zipper during the manufacturing process. It shows a thick nylon filament that has been twisted into a spiral around a flat needle. A central thread of many fibers runs up through the spiral, making the coil stronger. The teeth of the zipper have been made by flattening one side of the curves of the spiral. These teeth will interlock with a mirror arrangement of themselves, manufactured at the same time. The interlocking spirals are then sewn to tapes. Nylon zippers are cheaper and more flexible than metal zippers and can be made in colors to match the fabric.

One side of nylon filament zipper magnified 94 times.

The hooks and loops of Velcro magnified 2,408 times.

TOUCH FASTENERS

Velcro was invented by George de Mestral, a Swiss mountaineer, in 1948. He was inspired by the burrs that stuck to his clothes after a walk in the fields and decided to copy the idea by making tapes that would stick together with the press of a finger. One side of the fastener is made up of tiny hooks; the other is made of tiny loops. When the tapes are pressed together, enough hooks latch on to enough loops to hold the tapes in place. When the tapes are pulled apart, the flexible hooks are easily parted from the loops. Because one side of the tape is constructed the same way velvet is, and the other is similar to crochet, de Mestral combined the two words to create his trademark name Velcro.

The magnified photograph shows both sides of a Velcro fastener. It also tells us something about how Velcro is made. Both tapes are initially woven into loops, but the tape that will have the hooks is made from a heavier strand. Both kinds of tapes are woven out of flexible nylon threads under a heat lamp. The heat makes the threads harden into a permanent shape. After the shape is set, the heavier loops are cut on one side to form hooks.

Vision is the dominant sense in human beings. We have more nerves in our eyes than in all our other sense organs combined. Yet there are limits to what we can see. Objects that are too small or distant, events that happen too quickly or involve energy other than visible light, can be made visible with the help of special tools and the camera. Scientific photographs made this way add information about their subjects, and their images add to our appreciation of the beauty of nature and technology.

PHOTOS

INDEX

Italics indicate illustrations